TIMELESS WEAVE

ECHOES OF UNSPOKEN LOVE

shashi madhuri

BookLeaf Publishing

India | USA | UK

Made with ❤ on the BookLeaf Publishing Platform
www.bookleafpub.in
www.bookleafpub.com

Dedication

To the echoes of unspoken love, and the threads that bind us through time.

Preface

These poems are born from the quiet spaces between spoken words, from the echoes of memories that linger long after moments have passed, and from the intricate weave of human connection that transcends time and space. "Timeless Weave" is a collection of reflections on love, loss, longing, and the enduring power of the human heart.

The seeds of these verses were sown in moments of introspection, in the hushed stillness of twilight, and in the restless churn of unspoken emotions. They are inspired by the delicate dance of unspoken glances, the weight of unfulfilled desires, and the fragile beauty of memories that shimmer like fireflies in the night.

In these pages, you will find echoes of autumn's melancholy, the silent whispers of moonlit nights, and the turbulent depths of an ocean's soul. Each poem is an attempt to capture the essence of these fleeting moments, to give voice to the unspoken, and to explore the timeless tapestry of human experience.

I invite you to journey through these verses, to find solace in the shared language of the heart, and to discover the enduring threads that connect us all. May these poems serve as a mirror to your own soul, a gentle reminder of the beauty that resides within, and a testament to the enduring power of love and memory. "Timeless Weave" is not just a collection of words; it is an invitation to explore the silent landscapes of your own heart, to rediscover the beauty of unspoken connections, and to find solace in the enduring power of memory and love. I hope these poems resonate with you, and that you find a moment of peace within their pages.

Acknowledgements

This collection of poems, "Timeless Weave," would not have been possible without the support and inspiration of many.

1. Love's Illusion

Heart, so naïve, why do you stray?
Love is but a dream that fades away.
We mistook its whispers for life's sweet song,
Yet sorrow is where such dreams belong...

True companions are a fleeting grace,
A wager of love—a reckless chase.
The one I held with boundless pride,
Called their love mere kindness, belied...

Once, with a kiss upon my brow,
They vowed, "Your sorrows are mine from now."
Yet here I stand, beneath fate's reign,
Even my tale was not worth the pain...

Nights still echo their silent sighs,
Moonlit memories, deceiving ties.
Shadows dance where love once lay,
Fading footprints on time's cold clay...

What cruel jest does fate bestow,
To weave such warmth, then let it go?
A love so deep, yet built on sand,
Waves erase what hearts had planned...

Yet, foolish heart, you love again,
Chasing mirage through storm and rain.
For even when the wounds run deep,
Love's illusion still haunts my sleep.................

2. The Ocean Within

This heart, an ocean—endless, deep,
Cradles a thirst it cannot keep.
Time and again, the waves pull me
Into tides of memory—
Knowing well that salty seas
Can never set a soul at ease.

Still, I drift—
Floating, sinking, lost in time,
Bound to echoes left behind.
Storms arise, the waters roar,
Waves collide and shake my core,
Leaving me restless, longing more.

Yet, when I dive beyond the tide,
Past the turmoil, past the fear,
A single pearl of truth resides—
Untouched, luminous, crystal clear.
Sometimes, it soothes my weary soul,
Sometimes, my hands return with sand.

For years I've searched a sailor's call,
A guiding hand to lead me home.
But even he, in raging seas,
Has let his trusted oars fall free.

A silent heart, a whispered ache,
The ocean swells with every tear.
Yet here I stand, at fate's embrace,
Watching mist and doubt erase.
No thirst remains, no waiting lingers—
No distant shore, no restless fever.

Now my heart, a tranquil lake,
No longer yearns for paths unknown.
For if the journey calls my name,
It will find its way on its own.

3. Drenched in Love

Drenched in love,

My heart now trembles, in despair...

Regret lingers, as life has passed,

An exile's journey, nowhere there...

When waves of joy, like oceans deep ,

Arose to stir, my soul's own keep—

They crashed on rocks, of false design,

And turned to storms, beyond all sign.

Now thirst itself, feels like a dream,

A barren desert, life would seem...

My own true self, I cannot find,

In this vast space, where shadows bind.

Hands once held, now slip away,

Shattered dreams, in disarray...

And all that's left, within my core,

Are wounds that bleed, and evermore.

Yet in this void, a whisper's grace,

A strength within, I now embrace.

For even deserts, hold their peace,

And wounded hearts, find sweet release.

Though love may fade, and shadows stay,

My soul will rise, to find its way.

4. She, a Dream in Bloom

A stray lock graces her face so fair,
Like moonlight caught in midnight's snare.
Oh, to brush it with a lover's hand,
To pause the world at my command.

Her fragrance drifts, a silken sigh,
Like sandalwood 'neath starlit sky.
Oh, to steal that breath so sweet,
To let its whispers mine repeat.

She sways like vines in tender flight,
Bathed in dawn's embracing light.
Oh, to be the tree so tall,
To hold her close, to catch her fall.

Her voice—a koel's song at dawn,
A melody that lingers on.
Oh, to hear its echo deep,
To let it haunt the dreams I keep.

Her steps—a fawn on meadow's crest,
A fleeting waltz, a soft caress.
Oh, to chase where shadows play,
To wander where her whispers stay.

She, a vision, rare and bright,
A goddess bathed in heaven's light.
Oh, to dream of her always,
To lose myself within her gaze.

5. Let's Settle This

Who are we—
You to me, and I to you?
Strangers bound by fate's cruel whim,
Or echoes of a love once true?

Come, sit beside me in this hush,
Let's seek the answer, clear and bright.
Shall we mend what time has shattered,
Or let love vanish in the night?

Who will dare to break the silence,
To tear this fragile wall apart?
Shall we bury words unsaid forever,
Or lay them bare, heart to heart?

You hold grievances untold,
I bear wounds that never fade...
But who will voice their sorrow first,
Before our love is left to shade?

The road ahead is not too far,
If we dare to walk as one.
But who will take the first step now,
Before the chance is gone?

Our hands once fit like whispered vows,
Our dreams entwined, a sacred thread...
But silence grows like creeping vines,
Choking all we left unsaid.

So, come—let pride not pull us back,
Let love be our command.
For silence never healed a soul,
Let's reach- let's take a stand

6. O Lord, Grant Me Time Once More

O Lord, grant me time once more,
To weave my dolls' sweet dreams of yore.
Let laughter bloom like petals free,
And childhood's joys return to me.

Let marbles chime upon the ground,
Their echoes singing soft, profound.
Let skipping ropes in rhythm fly,
As golden days go dancing by.

Let me forget the world so wide,
And chase the breeze with arms spread wide.
In hide-and-seek, let me remain,
A whisper lost in time's refrain.

Bring back the light of endless noons,
The evenings kissed by silver moons.
Let paper boats set sail once more,

Upon the streams of days before.

For fleeting moments, lost too fast,
Are echoes wrapped in childhood's past.
O Lord, just once, I humbly pray,
Let stolen hours choose to stay.

7. A Sleepless Quest

Moon-spun thoughts on a night unblessed,
I wander, unbound, in their silent quest.
A faint smile flickers, a whispered plea,
Like moonlight veiled, eternally.

Your voice, a phantom, in shadows it weaves,
A chime of echoes, where slumber grieves.
Your gaze, a sun-kissed, molten art,
Melts the frozen edges of my heart.

Destiny's chisel, a sorrowful trace,
A patient vigil,love's empty space.
A summer bird, in thirst's despair,
For rain's sweet solace, beyond compare.

Yet, through the shadows, a star's soft gleam,
A fragile promise, within a dream.
Though sorrow lingers, and tears may fall,
Love's distant echo, will answer all.

8. A Symphony of Noise

The world hums loud in ceaseless streams,
Like rivers rushing through restless dreams.
Birdsongs weave through rustling trees,
Temple bells chime on the morning breeze.
Hymns arise in sacred lore—
Oh, the noise! It fills the core.
Oh, the noise! It evermore.

A child's laughter, soft yet bright,
Anklets dance in golden light.
Echoes of joy, a mother's call,
The clatter of pots in the kitchen hall.
Melodies hidden in everyday chore—
Oh, the noise! It fills the core.
Oh, the noise! It evermore.

Step outside, the city wakes,
A thousand voices, the silence breaks.
Blaring horns and hurried feet,

The restless pulse of crowded streets.
Sirens wail, the echoes soar—
Oh, the noise! It fills the core.
Oh, the noise! It evermore.

Yet in this clamor, listen deep,
A rhythm stirs, a song takes leap.
For noise and music, threads entwine,
It's how we shape their grand design.
A scattered sound, a tune once more,
Oh, the noise! It sings, it soars.

9. Cloud Dance

When golden rays,the sun's hot kiss,

Awaken waters, in misty bliss.

They rise, unbound, on currents free,

And drift aloft, in silent glee.

Soft, white whispers, weave and twine,

Then darken, as they upward climb.

Gathering strength in skies so vast,

Till mountains halt their soaring cast.

Thunder drums, the heavens weep,

And rain descends, in torrents deep.

The parched earth drinks, with eager thirst,

As rivers surge, from slumber burst.

They leap and twirl, in joyful flight,

Carving pathways, day and night.

Rushing, dancing, wild and bold,

To meet the sea, their story told.

Yet soon again, the sun's bright reign,

Begins the cycle, once again.

For every drop, that dares to soar,

Returns to kiss, the waiting shore.

10. Night's Silver Secrets

In night's deep hush,where shadows creep,

Moonlight weaves a world of sleep.

A silver stream, a murmured sigh,

A fleeting dream, that drifts nearby.

Beneath the trees, where shadows twine,

Branches sway, like lovers' sign.

Secrets whispered, soft and low,

In rustling sighs, the night winds know.

Vines embrace, in drowsy grace,

Leaf to leaf, a close embrace.

Lost in dreams, both joy and pain,

In whispered truths, that still remain.

With half-closed eyes, the birds observe,

The moon's cold dance, the sky's soft curve.

Dew-kissed grass, in silent grace,

Awaits the dawn, in time and space.

Some speak, some listen, shadows blend,

Where nature's heart, words transcend.

Then, as the sky begins to pale,

The silver secrets start to fail.

A fading echo, soft and light,

Lost in the promise of morning's might.

11. Soulful Eyes

Blushing soft, then swiftly veiled,

Glistening bright, where joy has sailed.

Drenched in laughter, wild and bold,

Or wine-dark depths, a story told.

They open wide, then softly close

Like twilight petals, in repose.

Heavy with dreams, or thoughts untold,

A world unseen, in moments scrolled.

They guard their truths, with subtle art,

Yet glimpse a soul, a beating heart.

They smile in sorrow, weep in glee,

A tide of whispers, wild and free.

If you can read, they weave a rhyme,

Of love and loss, in passing time.

Mirrors of soul, a boundless sea,

A universe held, for you and me.

And when they meet, in silent grace,

Two worlds collide, in time and space.

A spark ignites, a fleeting fire,

A moment held, a deep desire.

12. Timeless Weave

Was it mere chance, a fleeting tide,

That brought your soul, to walk beside?

Or did fate's hand, in whispers deep,

Our meeting write, while worlds asleep?

In teeming crowds, why only you,

A stranger's face, yet felt so true?

Some stand close, yet hearts remain,

Uncharted lands, in sun and rain.

Perhaps a thread, from ages flown,

A silent vow, on starlight sown.

For hearts don't bind, without a cause,

Nor weave a bond, past mortal laws.

All reason fades, no answers stay,

This tangled maze, where shadows play.

Yet when your hand, in mine finds hold,

The world transforms, in stories told.

And in that touch, a memory stirs,

A distant echo, time confers.

A sense of knowing, deep and vast,

A love that's found, and meant to last.

13. Heart's Phantom

You knock so softly, heart's faint chime,

Then vanish, lost to passing time.

Your laughter's echo, a whispered grace,

Yet lips stay sealed, in empty space.

Like dawn's gold flood, or dusk's red fire,

You steal my breath, ignite desire.

You stir my soul, in silent play,

Then leave me breathless, far away.

Fragrant as blooms, on windswept trail,

You drift, you sail, beyond the veil.

Through nights of longing, songs unsung,

Why chase the moon, with heart unstrung?

You weave a spell, a silken snare,

Then leave me lost, in thin, cold air.

And as you turn, with heart of stone,

Why is my heart, you claim your own?

Yet in the stillness, I perceive,

The fragile truths you won't believe.

A flicker of warmth, a hidden tear,

A silent longing, held so dear.

14. Whispers of the River

I watched a river, on its flight,

Leaping, laughing, in golden light.

Swaying softly, wild and free,

Twirling, blushing, in ecstasy.

It kissed the stones, then slipped away,

A lover's touch, in gentle sway.

Some it whispered, secrets deep,

Some it cradled, in its sweep.

Yet fierce or fleeting, swift or slow,

No matter how its currents flow,

When it meets the vast, unending sea,

It yields, unbound, eternally.

And in its song, a truth I find,

A tender heart, can shape mankind.

For oceans bend, to love's embrace,

And gentle souls, still find their place.

For in that yielding, strength resides,

A silent wisdom, nature guides.

To let go, not to lose, but gain,

And find release, from earthly chain.

15. The Gliding Dream

In scented air, with steps so light,

Drifting soft, as moonlit white,

If only I could near them glide,

Then night would bloom, with dawn inside.

Like sandalwood, my breath's soft grace,

A lingering hush, in time and space,

If only I could cross their path,

Then winds would sing, a sacred wrath.

Like rivers twirling, wild and shy,

Beneath the vast, celestial sky,

If only I could waltz and soar,

Then waves would envy, evermore.

Like kites that chase, the rushing breeze,

Dancing high, with joyful ease,

If only I could reach their hand,

Then clouds would blush, across the land.

Like morning's blush, on petal's fold,

crimson sigh, a story told,

If only I could touch their light,

Then sun would linger, through the night.

Like moonlight draped, in silver thread,

A veil of stars, above my head,

If only I could reach their door,

Then love's lost tale, would live once more.

16. Veiled Echoes

Something lingered, a silent plea...

The hush in your eyes, the glance turned low,
The blush that bloomed, when my name would flow.

And in rooms where whispers crept,
You'd slip away, where secrets slept.

Something lingered, a moonlit sigh...
On shadowed eaves, where leaves would lie,

You wove your breath, in silent grace,
Shielding the flame, in time and space.

Startled by echoes, soft and deep,
Yet watched me close, while others sleep.

Something lingered, a sacred veil...
A soul untouched, a love so pale.

No eyes had traced, her tender face,
Yet hearts had danced, in hidden space.

And when I saw her, one last gleam,
She stayed veiled, a whispered dream.

Something lingered, a fading trace,
A silent whisper, time can't erase.

A world of whispers, soft and near,
Where hearts could speak, without a fear.

A bond that time, could not erase,
A silent language, in time and space.

17. Twilight's Grace

Years ago, my love, when eyes first met,

Youth's golden aura, around me set.

A divine shimmer, in twilight's grace,

A tender blush, time couldn't chase.

A hundred seasons, since we began,

Silver threads now, where gold once ran.

Colors dimmed, and steps grew slow,

Smiles once bright, a gentler glow.

The dream you spun, in starlit nights—

If I stand now, in fading lights...

Tell me, my love, with heart so true,

Will you still hold me, as you once knew?

Will your eyes still shine, with love's soft flame?

Will you still whisper, my cherished name?

For love's true essence, knows no age,

But deepens, on life's weathered page.

And in each line, etched by time's hand,

Our souls entwined, will ever stand.

So fear not, love, my heart will see,

The timeless beauty, you are to me.

18. Shared Song

Joy is not found............

where words alone,
Fall on ears, to hearts unknown.

Not in longing's piercing dart,
That wounds one soul, while others part.

Not in tears that stain the night,
Nor fading steps, lost to the light.

Not in paths, where hearts divide,
Seeking solace, cast aside.

Joy is found............

where voices blend,
A melody, where echoes mend.

Where gazes meet, and sighs confess,
Love's tender ache, in soft caress.

To weep as one, upon your breast,
To find my peace, in shared unrest.

To walk as one, through sun and shade,
With hands entwined, and unafraid.

And if we tire, let it be,
Held in arms, where peace runs free.

And in that quiet, we will find,
A sanctuary, for heart and mind.

Where fragile truths, are safe to share,
And burdens lightened, by our care.

For true joy blooms, where souls unite,
In shared embrace, and gentle light.

19. Traces in Time

Not whole, yet not in vain's cold hold,

If my tale's thread, could still unfold.

A whispered name, on windswept breeze,

A song unsung, through shadowed trees.

The world's cruel hand, would not allow,

Our love's fierce bloom, to gently bow.

Yet in my soul, your image lies,

A dream's embrace, beneath starlit skies.

They say my charm, still softly glows,

A fleeting grace, where memory flows.

If your voice had called, my name's sweet sound,

The world would know, where love was found.

Legends speak, of love's pure fire,

Of hearts that burned, with deep desire.

Had passion flowed, in rivers vast,

I'd cross the stones, where shadows cast.

The moon bears scars, yet shines so bright,

A celestial beacon, in darkest night.

If love were freed, from worldly chains,

And measured not, by fleeting gains...

And in the silence, where dreams reside,

Our love's soft echo, will abide.

Though fate's harsh hand, may keep us apart,

Our souls will meet, within the heart.

For love's true story, knows no end,

But lives on, where memories blend.

20. Fading Frames

If love was never meant to bloom,

Then why unearth, my image from its tomb?

Why did your gaze, upon it stay,

Lost in a moment, far away?

Why did you brush, the dust's soft trace,

With tender hands, that time erased?

Why did you mend, its tilted frame,

A relic touched, by fading flame?

Why did your eyes, seek hues to mend,

Only to blur, where sorrows blend?

And seeing your face, within the glass,

Why did you blush, as moments pass?

But even now, you're just as fair,

Silver strands, in moonlight's care.

If love was never meant to be,

Why do you stand, and gaze at me?

And in that gaze, a truth unfolds,

A love that time, can't break or hold.

For memories bloom, where hearts still yearn,

A silent flame, that will not burn.

Though fate may part, and shadows fall,

Our love's reflection, answers all.

21. Silent Glimpses

The mirror, my witness, day by day,

Yet in his gaze, I found a hidden way.

Perhaps love's whisper, found him first,

For every glance, a silent thirst.

At one street's end, his dwelling stood,

Mine at the other, in solitude.

Yet unseen paths, of fate's design,

He found a way, to intertwine.

Perched on rooftops, eaves so high,

Chasing glimpses, 'neath the sky.

In summer's heat, with breath held tight,

He burned beneath, the midday light.

A hundred times, he'd pass my door,

With kite or string, excuses bore.

Yet never dared, to step within,

Where love's faint shadow, lingered thin.

Was he too young, or I too old?

Did time conspire, a story told?

For love knows not, of years or days,

But sways with whispers, dreams, and ways.

My temple lay, along his stride,

Where he would pause, but not abide.

He changed his path, his time, his call,

Yet left a greeting, soft and small.

And still... Why did he call me, beautiful?

And in the silence, questions bloom,

A heart's lament, within the room.

Did fear or doubt, his spirit bind?

Or was it love, of a different kind?

A love unspoken, a silent plea,

An echo lost, eternally.

22. The Dark Corner

That shadowed nook, so cold, so deep,
Still haunts my mind, disturbs my sleep.

Even my own shadow fled away,
While silence echoed loud that day.

Just the thought still chills my skin,
A fear long buried, yet deep within.

Alone in body, yet crowded in mind,
Echoes of whispers, eerie, unkind.

Only the voices of night remained,
As the hush of darkness softly reigned.

Just the thought still chills my skin,
A fear long buried, yet deep within.

By day, that space felt warm, my own,

But night would steal its comfort known.

The veil of dusk would shift its hue,
And turn the safe into the new.

Just the thought still chills my skin,
A fear long buried, yet deep within.

The bending boughs in whispers called,
Like unseen hands behind me sprawled.

A creeping voice, a silent stare,
A pull into the midnight air.

Just the thought still chills my skin,
A fear long buried, yet deep within.

No soul could hear my silent cry,
This childhood ghost refused to die.

For in my yard, it stood alone—
That dreaded, dark, forsaken zone.

Just the thought still chills my skin,
A fear long buried, yet deep within.

23. Towers of Glasses

Windows once flung wide and free,

Invited laughter, sun's decree.

A gateway where, from kitchens near,

Aromas danced, on whispers clear.

A perch for tales, in light's embrace,

A hidden world, in time and space.

A secret door, for late night flight,

From father's ire, in fading light.

Now high above, where towers rise,

They hang like eyes, in distant skies.

No earth to touch, no moon to claim,

Half-closed they stay, a silent shame.

Crowded close, yet souls apart,

No stolen glance, no warming heart.

Once bridges built, to lives so nigh,

Now just cold glass, where shadows lie.

Yet through the pane, a hope remains,

A flicker of warmth, through falling rains.

For even glass, can catch a gleam,

And hearts can mend, a broken dream.

Though walls may rise, and distance grow,

A gentle light, will softly glow.

52

24. Reckoning's Price

Come, let us weigh, the worth of days,

Of whispered dreams, and lost refrains,

Of silent sighs, and love's soft maze—

And I shall pay...

Of dawn's first kiss, so light and fair,

Of velvet dusk, and moonlit air,

Of stars that danced, in silver snare—

Let's name their price...

And I shall pay...

Of hands entwined, then torn away,

Of echoes deep, where memories lay,

Of love that strayed, yet held its sway—

Let's count the cost...

And I shall pay...

I know, like time, you slip and fade,

Yet priceless is, the bond we made,

Come, name the debt, my soul must trade—

And I shall pay... and I shall pay...

For even loss, a treasure holds,

A story etched, in hearts untold.

And though the price, may cause me pain,

The love we shared, will still remain.

So name the debt, and I will see

The worth of you, eternally.

25. Leaves of Longing

Now autumn's chill, where spring once reigned,

My whispers cast, a shadow stained.

Silence thrives, where words took flight,

And love dissolved, in fading light.

I longed to meet, a moment's grace,

Yet fate's cruel hand, erased your trace.

Memories gleam, like fireflies' spark,

Then vanish deep, into the dark.

A storm's unrest, within me churns,

A tide unspoken, where longing burns.

Yet here I stand, as seasons wane,

Chasing a dream, through grief and pain.

But in this stillness, I shall find

A gentle peace, for heart and mind.

For even autumn, holds its grace,

And memories bloom, in time and space.

Though love's bright flame, may cease to glow,

My soul will learn, to softly flow.

26. Rainbow

In the distant sky, so vast and free,
The same sun glows, the moon, the sea.

Stars shimmer soft in night's embrace,
While drifting clouds begin their chase.

Who knows when skies will bend and break,
When restless winds the earth will wake?

A whisper stirs, a hush so light,
Then raindrops dance in pure delight.

The vast blue waits with longing eyes,
For heaven's tears to cleanse the skies.

A single drop, a tender call,
Then rhythm sways as showers fall.

The rainbow blooms in colors bright,
A bridge of dreams, of hope, of light.

As monsoon's song begins to play,
It washes every pain away.

27. A Hope Still Remains

Your touch, like breath, revived my soul,
Restoring pieces once left whole.
If love's a debt I've yet to pay,
Your grace outshines what words can say.

The ache within still haunts me deep,
My heart still longs, my dreams still weep.
Fate may knock upon my door,
Yet still, I wait—to walk once more.

If loving you defied what's right,
I'd bow again in heaven's light.
Alone I stand, yet hope remains,
A whisper soft—you'll come again.

The stars still trace your name in light,
A silent prayer in endless night.
The wind still hums your melody,

A tune of love, a song of me.

Time may shift, the seasons fade,
Yet love stands strong, unbent, unfrayed.
So if the road should lead you near,
Know my heart still waits right here.